50 Healthy Breakfast Recipes for Home

By: Kelly Johnson

Table of Contents

- Quinoa and Black Bean Salad
- Mediterranean Chickpea Salad
- Turkey and Avocado Lettuce Wraps
- Sweet Potato and Black Bean Burrito Bowl
- Grilled Chicken and Veggie Skewers
- Spinach and Feta Stuffed Chicken Breast
- Thai Peanut Noodle Salad
- Cauliflower Rice Stir-Fry
- Greek Yogurt Chicken Salad
- Zucchini Noodles with Pesto
- Lentil and Vegetable Soup
- Roasted Veggie and Hummus Wrap
- Edamame and Corn Salad
- Chickpea and Spinach Stuffed Pita
- Turkey and Spinach Breakfast Casserole
- Baked Salmon with Lemon and Dill
- Broccoli and Cheddar Stuffed Sweet Potatoes
- Avocado and Egg Breakfast Bowl
- Spicy Black Bean and Sweet Potato Tacos
- Sweet Potato and Avocado Breakfast Tacos
- Fresh Fruit Salad with Mint
- Almond Flour Muffins with Blueberries
- Veggie-Packed Quiche with a Sweet Potato Crust
- Greek Salad with Chicken
- Tofu and Veggie Stir-Fry
- Baked Apples with Cinnamon and Walnuts
- Protein-Packed Breakfast Smoothie with Spinach
- Roasted Veggie and Hummus Wrap
- Sweet Potato Hash with Poached Eggs
- Chia Seed Pudding with Almond Milk
- Whole Wheat Banana Pancakes
- Green Smoothie with Spinach and Apple

- Berry and Spinach Smoothie Bowl
- Cottage Cheese with Pineapple and Almonds
- Kale and Mushroom Frittata
- Almond Butter and Banana Smoothie
- Whole Grain French Toast with Fresh Berries
- Apple and Walnut Oat Muffins
- Spicy Black Bean and Sweet Potato Tacos
- Veggie-Stuffed Omelette
- Baked Eggplant with Tomato and Basil
- Avocado Toast with Cherry Tomatoes
- Cauliflower Rice Stir-Fry with Eggs
- Smoked Salmon and Cream Cheese on Whole Grain Bagels
- Chickpea and Spinach Stuffed Pita
- Sweet Potato and Avocado Breakfast Tacos
- Greek Salad with Chicken
- Apple and Walnut Oat Muffins
- Spicy Black Bean and Sweet Potato Tacos
- Veggie-Stuffed Omelette

Quinoa and Black Bean Salad

Ingredients:

- **For the Salad:**
    - 1 cup quinoa, rinsed
    - 1 1/2 cups water or vegetable broth
    - 1 can (15 oz) black beans, drained and rinsed
    - 1 cup cherry tomatoes, halved
    - 1 cup corn kernels (fresh, frozen, or canned, drained)
    - 1/2 cup red bell pepper, diced
    - 1/4 cup red onion, finely diced
    - 1/4 cup fresh cilantro, chopped
- **For the Dressing:**
    - 1/4 cup olive oil
    - 2 tablespoons lime juice (about 1 lime)
    - 1 tablespoon red wine vinegar
    - 1 clove garlic, minced
    - 1 teaspoon ground cumin
    - 1/2 teaspoon chili powder
    - Salt and pepper, to taste

Instructions:

1. **Cook the Quinoa:**
    - In a medium saucepan, bring 1 1/2 cups water or vegetable broth to a boil.
    - Add the rinsed quinoa, reduce the heat to low, cover, and simmer for 15 minutes, or until the quinoa is tender and the liquid is absorbed.
    - Remove from heat and let it sit, covered, for 5 minutes. Fluff with a fork and let cool.
2. **Prepare the Salad Ingredients:**
    - In a large bowl, combine the cooked quinoa, black beans, cherry tomatoes, corn, red bell pepper, red onion, and fresh cilantro.
3. **Make the Dressing:**
    - In a small bowl or jar, whisk together olive oil, lime juice, red wine vinegar, minced garlic, ground cumin, chili powder, salt, and pepper.
4. **Combine and Serve:**
    - Pour the dressing over the quinoa mixture and toss to coat evenly.
    - Taste and adjust seasoning if needed.
5. **Chill and Serve:**
    - Chill the salad in the refrigerator for at least 30 minutes to allow flavors to meld. Serve cold or at room temperature.

Enjoy your nutritious and flavorful Quinoa and Black Bean Salad!

Mediterranean Chickpea Salad

Ingredients:

- **For the Salad:**
    - 1 can (15 oz) chickpeas, drained and rinsed
    - 1 cup cherry tomatoes, halved
    - 1/2 cucumber, diced
    - 1/4 red onion, finely diced
    - 1/4 cup Kalamata olives, pitted and sliced
    - 1/4 cup crumbled feta cheese
    - 1/4 cup fresh parsley, chopped
- **For the Dressing:**
    - 1/4 cup extra-virgin olive oil
    - 2 tablespoons red wine vinegar
    - 1 tablespoon lemon juice (about 1/2 lemon)
    - 1 clove garlic, minced
    - 1 teaspoon dried oregano
    - Salt and pepper, to taste

Instructions:

1. **Prepare the Salad Ingredients:**
    - In a large bowl, combine the chickpeas, cherry tomatoes, cucumber, red onion, Kalamata olives, feta cheese, and fresh parsley.
2. **Make the Dressing:**
    - In a small bowl or jar, whisk together the olive oil, red wine vinegar, lemon juice, minced garlic, dried oregano, salt, and pepper until well combined.
3. **Combine and Serve:**
    - Pour the dressing over the salad and toss gently to coat all ingredients evenly.
4. **Chill (Optional):**
    - For the best flavor, let the salad chill in the refrigerator for at least 30 minutes before serving.
5. **Serve:**
    - Serve chilled or at room temperature as a refreshing and healthy lunch or side dish.

Enjoy your Mediterranean Chickpea Salad!

Turkey and Avocado Lettuce Wraps

Ingredients:

- **For the Wraps:**
    - 1 pound ground turkey
    - 1 tablespoon olive oil
    - 1 small onion, finely diced
    - 2 cloves garlic, minced
    - 1 teaspoon ground cumin
    - 1 teaspoon paprika
    - 1/2 teaspoon chili powder (optional)
    - Salt and pepper, to taste
    - 1 avocado, sliced
    - 1 cup cherry tomatoes, halved
    - 1/4 cup fresh cilantro, chopped (optional)
    - 12 large lettuce leaves (e.g., Romaine or Butter Lettuce)
- **For the Sauce (optional):**
    - 2 tablespoons Greek yogurt
    - 1 tablespoon lime juice
    - 1 teaspoon honey or maple syrup
    - Salt and pepper, to taste

Instructions:

1. **Cook the Turkey:**
    - Heat olive oil in a skillet over medium heat.
    - Add diced onion and cook until softened, about 3-4 minutes.
    - Add minced garlic and cook for another 1 minute.
    - Add ground turkey, cumin, paprika, chili powder (if using), salt, and pepper. Cook until the turkey is browned and cooked through, breaking it apart with a spoon, about 7-10 minutes.
    - Remove from heat and set aside.
2. **Prepare the Sauce (optional):**
    - In a small bowl, mix Greek yogurt, lime juice, honey or maple syrup, salt, and pepper. Adjust seasoning to taste.
3. **Assemble the Wraps:**
    - To each lettuce leaf, add a spoonful of the cooked turkey mixture.
    - Top with avocado slices, cherry tomatoes, and chopped cilantro if desired.
    - Drizzle with the optional sauce or serve on the side.
4. **Serve:**
    - Serve immediately as a fresh, low-carb lunch or appetizer.

Enjoy your flavorful Turkey and Avocado Lettuce Wraps!

Sweet Potato and Black Bean Burrito Bowl

Ingredients:

- **For the Bowl:**
    - 1 large sweet potato, peeled and diced
    - 1 tablespoon olive oil
    - 1 teaspoon chili powder
    - 1/2 teaspoon ground cumin
    - Salt and pepper, to taste
    - 1 can (15 oz) black beans, drained and rinsed
    - 1 cup cooked brown rice or quinoa
    - 1 cup corn kernels (fresh, frozen, or canned, drained)
    - 1 avocado, sliced
    - 1 cup cherry tomatoes, halved
    - 1/4 cup fresh cilantro, chopped
- **For the Dressing (optional):**
    - 1/4 cup Greek yogurt or sour cream
    - 1 tablespoon lime juice (about 1/2 lime)
    - 1/2 teaspoon garlic powder
    - Salt and pepper, to taste

Instructions:

1. **Roast the Sweet Potatoes:**
    - Preheat your oven to 400°F (200°C). Line a baking sheet with parchment paper.
    - Toss the diced sweet potato with olive oil, chili powder, cumin, salt, and pepper.
    - Spread the sweet potato in a single layer on the baking sheet.
    - Roast for 20-25 minutes, or until tender and slightly caramelized, stirring halfway through. Allow to cool slightly.
2. **Prepare the Dressing (optional):**
    - In a small bowl, mix Greek yogurt, lime juice, garlic powder, salt, and pepper until smooth. Adjust seasoning as needed.
3. **Assemble the Burrito Bowl:**
    - In serving bowls, layer the cooked brown rice or quinoa as the base.
    - Top with roasted sweet potatoes, black beans, corn, cherry tomatoes, and avocado slices.
    - Drizzle with the optional dressing or serve on the side.
4. **Garnish and Serve:**
    - Garnish with fresh cilantro.
    - Serve immediately and enjoy your hearty and nutritious Sweet Potato and Black Bean Burrito Bowl!

Grilled Chicken and Veggie Skewers

Ingredients:

- **For the Skewers:**
    - 1 pound boneless, skinless chicken breasts or thighs, cut into bite-sized pieces
    - 1 red bell pepper, cut into chunks
    - 1 green bell pepper, cut into chunks
    - 1 medium onion, cut into chunks
    - 1 zucchini, sliced into rounds
    - 1 cup cherry tomatoes
    - 2 tablespoons olive oil
    - 1 tablespoon lemon juice
    - 2 cloves garlic, minced
    - 1 teaspoon dried oregano
    - 1 teaspoon smoked paprika
    - Salt and pepper, to taste
- **For Garnish (optional):**
    - Fresh parsley, chopped
    - Lemon wedges

Instructions:

1. **Marinate the Chicken:**
    - In a bowl, mix olive oil, lemon juice, minced garlic, dried oregano, smoked paprika, salt, and pepper.
    - Add chicken pieces and toss to coat. Marinate in the refrigerator for at least 30 minutes, or up to 2 hours for more flavor.
2. **Prepare the Vegetables:**
    - In a separate bowl, toss bell peppers, onion, zucchini, and cherry tomatoes with a bit of olive oil, salt, and pepper.
3. **Assemble the Skewers:**
    - Preheat your grill to medium-high heat.
    - Thread marinated chicken pieces and vegetables alternately onto skewers. If using wooden skewers, soak them in water for 30 minutes beforehand to prevent burning.
4. **Grill the Skewers:**
    - Place the skewers on the grill and cook for 10-15 minutes, turning occasionally, until the chicken is cooked through (internal temperature of 165°F or 74°C) and the vegetables are tender.
5. **Serve:**
    - Remove from the grill and let cool slightly.
    - Garnish with fresh parsley and lemon wedges if desired.

Enjoy your flavorful and colorful Grilled Chicken and Veggie Skewers!

Spinach and Feta Stuffed Chicken Breast
Ingredients:

For the Stuffed Chicken:

4 boneless, skinless chicken breasts
1 cup fresh spinach, chopped
1/2 cup crumbled feta cheese
2 cloves garlic, minced
1/4 cup sun-dried tomatoes, chopped (optional)
1 tablespoon olive oil
1/2 teaspoon dried oregano
Salt and pepper, to taste
For Cooking:

1 tablespoon olive oil
1/2 cup chicken broth or white wine
Instructions:

Prepare the Filling:

In a bowl, mix chopped spinach, crumbled feta cheese, minced garlic, and sun-dried tomatoes (if using).
Prepare the Chicken:

Preheat your oven to 375°F (190°C).
Place each chicken breast between two sheets of plastic wrap. Pound with a meat mallet or rolling pin until about 1/2 inch thick.
Season both sides of the chicken breasts with salt, pepper, and dried oregano.
Stuff the Chicken:

Spoon the spinach and feta mixture onto one side of each chicken breast.
Fold the chicken over the filling and secure with toothpicks or kitchen twine.
Sear the Chicken:

Heat olive oil in a large ovenproof skillet over medium-high heat.
Add the stuffed chicken breasts and cook for 3-4 minutes per side, or until golden brown.
Bake:

Transfer the skillet to the preheated oven and bake for 15-20 minutes, or until the chicken reaches an internal temperature of 165°F (74°C) and the filling is hot.
Serve:

Remove from the oven and let the chicken rest for 5 minutes before slicing. Serve with a side of your choice, such as roasted vegetables or a fresh salad. Enjoy your flavorful and satisfying Spinach and Feta Stuffed Chicken Breast!

Thai Peanut Noodle Salad

Ingredients:

- **For the Salad:**
    - 8 oz rice noodles or soba noodles
    - 1 cup shredded carrots
    - 1 cup red bell pepper, thinly sliced
    - 1 cup cucumber, julienned
    - 1/2 cup edamame (shelled)
    - 1/4 cup chopped fresh cilantro
    - 1/4 cup chopped peanuts (optional, for garnish)
    - 2 green onions, thinly sliced (optional)
- **For the Peanut Dressing:**
    - 1/4 cup creamy peanut butter
    - 2 tablespoons soy sauce or tamari
    - 2 tablespoons rice vinegar
    - 1 tablespoon honey or maple syrup
    - 1 tablespoon sesame oil
    - 1 clove garlic, minced
    - 1 teaspoon grated fresh ginger
    - 1-2 tablespoons water (to thin the dressing, as needed)

Instructions:

1. **Cook the Noodles:**
    - Cook the rice noodles or soba noodles according to package instructions. Drain and rinse under cold water to cool.
2. **Prepare the Vegetables:**
    - While the noodles are cooking, prepare the shredded carrots, sliced bell pepper, julienned cucumber, and edamame.
3. **Make the Peanut Dressing:**
    - In a bowl or blender, whisk together peanut butter, soy sauce, rice vinegar, honey, sesame oil, minced garlic, and grated ginger.
    - Add water a little at a time until the dressing reaches your desired consistency.
4. **Assemble the Salad:**
    - In a large bowl, combine the cooked noodles, shredded carrots, bell pepper, cucumber, edamame, and chopped cilantro.
    - Pour the peanut dressing over the salad and toss gently to coat everything evenly.
5. **Garnish and Serve:**
    - Garnish with chopped peanuts and green onions if desired.
    - Serve immediately or chill in the refrigerator for 30 minutes to let the flavors meld.

Enjoy your refreshing and flavorful Thai Peanut Noodle Salad!

Cauliflower Rice Stir-Fry

Ingredients:

- **For the Stir-Fry:**
    - 1 large head of cauliflower (or 4 cups pre-grated cauliflower rice)
    - 2 tablespoons olive oil or sesame oil
    - 1 cup mixed vegetables (e.g., bell peppers, carrots, snap peas), diced
    - 2 cloves garlic, minced
    - 1 tablespoon fresh ginger, grated
    - 2 eggs, beaten
    - 1/4 cup soy sauce or tamari
    - 1 tablespoon rice vinegar
    - 1 teaspoon sesame oil (optional)
    - 2 green onions, sliced (for garnish)
    - Sesame seeds (optional, for garnish)

Instructions:

1. **Prepare the Cauliflower Rice:**
    - If using a whole cauliflower, remove the leaves and stem, and cut it into florets. Pulse in a food processor until it resembles rice grains.
2. **Cook the Vegetables:**
    - Heat olive oil or sesame oil in a large skillet or wok over medium-high heat.
    - Add diced vegetables and stir-fry for 3-4 minutes until tender-crisp.
3. **Add Aromatics:**
    - Add minced garlic and grated ginger to the skillet, cooking for another 1 minute until fragrant.
4. **Cook the Cauliflower Rice:**
    - Push the vegetables to one side of the skillet. Add a little more oil if needed, then add the cauliflower rice.
    - Stir-fry for 5-7 minutes, or until the cauliflower is tender and slightly golden.
5. **Add Eggs:**
    - Push the cauliflower rice and vegetables to the side of the skillet.
    - Pour beaten eggs into the empty side and scramble until fully cooked, then mix with the cauliflower rice and vegetables.
6. **Season and Serve:**
    - Stir in soy sauce, rice vinegar, and sesame oil (if using).
    - Garnish with sliced green onions and sesame seeds if desired.

Enjoy your healthy and flavorful Cauliflower Rice Stir-Fry!

Greek Yogurt Chicken Salad

Ingredients:

- **For the Salad:**
    - 2 cups cooked chicken, diced (such as rotisserie chicken or poached chicken breast)
    - 1/2 cup plain Greek yogurt
    - 1 tablespoon Dijon mustard
    - 1 tablespoon lemon juice (about 1/2 lemon)
    - 1 celery stalk, finely diced
    - 1/4 cup red onion, finely diced
    - 1/4 cup fresh parsley, chopped
    - 1/4 cup sliced almonds or chopped walnuts (optional)
    - Salt and pepper, to taste
- **For Serving (optional):**
    - Lettuce leaves or whole grain bread

Instructions:

1. **Prepare the Dressing:**
    - In a large bowl, mix Greek yogurt, Dijon mustard, and lemon juice until smooth.
2. **Combine Ingredients:**
    - Add diced chicken, celery, red onion, and fresh parsley to the bowl.
    - Stir until everything is well coated with the dressing.
3. **Add Nuts (Optional):**
    - Fold in sliced almonds or chopped walnuts if using.
4. **Season:**
    - Season with salt and pepper to taste. Mix well.
5. **Serve:**
    - Serve the chicken salad on lettuce leaves or as a sandwich filling on whole grain bread.

Enjoy your healthy Greek Yogurt Chicken Salad!

Zucchini Noodles with Pesto

Ingredients:

- **For the Zucchini Noodles:**
    - 4 medium zucchinis, spiralized into noodles
    - 1 tablespoon olive oil
    - Salt and pepper, to taste
- **For the Pesto:**
    - 1 cup fresh basil leaves
    - 1/4 cup pine nuts (or walnuts)
    - 1/4 cup grated Parmesan cheese
    - 2 cloves garlic
    - 1/4 cup extra-virgin olive oil
    - 1 tablespoon lemon juice
    - Salt and pepper, to taste

Instructions:

1. **Prepare the Pesto:**
    - In a food processor or blender, combine basil leaves, pine nuts, Parmesan cheese, and garlic.
    - Pulse until finely chopped.
    - With the processor running, slowly drizzle in the olive oil until the mixture is smooth and creamy.
    - Add lemon juice, salt, and pepper to taste. Pulse to combine.
2. **Cook the Zucchini Noodles:**
    - Heat olive oil in a large skillet over medium heat.
    - Add the spiralized zucchini noodles and cook for 2-3 minutes, stirring occasionally, until just tender. Be careful not to overcook; you want them to retain some crunch.
    - Season with salt and pepper.
3. **Combine and Serve:**
    - Remove the skillet from heat and toss the zucchini noodles with the pesto until evenly coated.
    - Serve immediately, garnished with extra Parmesan cheese or fresh basil if desired.

Enjoy your healthy and delicious Zucchini Noodles with Pesto!

Lentil and Vegetable Soup

Ingredients:

- **For the Soup:**
    - 1 tablespoon olive oil
    - 1 onion, diced
    - 2 cloves garlic, minced
    - 2 carrots, diced
    - 2 celery stalks, diced
    - 1 red bell pepper, diced
    - 1 cup dried green or brown lentils, rinsed and drained
    - 1 can (14.5 oz) diced tomatoes
    - 6 cups vegetable broth or chicken broth
    - 1 cup green beans, cut into bite-sized pieces
    - 1 cup spinach or kale, chopped
    - 1 teaspoon dried thyme
    - 1 teaspoon dried basil
    - 1 bay leaf
    - 1 teaspoon cumin (optional)
    - Salt and pepper, to taste
    - 1 tablespoon lemon juice (optional)

Instructions:

1. **Sauté the Aromatics:**
    - Heat olive oil in a large pot over medium heat.
    - Add diced onion and cook until softened, about 5 minutes.
    - Add minced garlic and cook for another 1 minute until fragrant.
2. **Add Vegetables:**
    - Stir in diced carrots, celery, and red bell pepper. Cook for about 5 minutes, stirring occasionally.
3. **Add Lentils and Broth:**
    - Add the rinsed lentils, diced tomatoes (with their juice), and vegetable broth to the pot.
    - Stir in dried thyme, dried basil, bay leaf, and cumin (if using).
    - Bring the mixture to a boil, then reduce the heat to low and cover.
4. **Simmer:**
    - Simmer the soup for about 25-30 minutes, or until the lentils are tender and the vegetables are cooked through.
5. **Add Green Beans and Greens:**
    - Stir in green beans and cook for another 5-7 minutes until the beans are tender.
    - Add spinach or kale and cook for an additional 2 minutes, until wilted.
6. **Season and Serve:**

- - Remove the bay leaf. Taste the soup and season with salt and pepper as needed.
  - Stir in lemon juice if desired for added brightness.
  - Serve hot, and enjoy!

This Lentil and Vegetable Soup is both filling and nutritious, making it a perfect choice for a comforting meal.

Roasted Veggie and Hummus Wrap

Ingredients:

- **For the Roasted Veggies:**
    - 1 red bell pepper, sliced
    - 1 zucchini, sliced
    - 1 cup cherry tomatoes, halved
    - 1 red onion, sliced
    - 1 tablespoon olive oil
    - 1 teaspoon dried oregano
    - 1/2 teaspoon garlic powder
    - Salt and pepper, to taste
- **For the Wrap:**
    - 4 large whole wheat or spinach tortillas
    - 1 cup hummus (store-bought or homemade)
    - 1 cup baby spinach or arugula
    - 1/4 cup crumbled feta cheese (optional)
    - 1 avocado, sliced (optional)
    - Lemon wedges (optional, for serving)

Instructions:

1. **Roast the Vegetables:**
    - Preheat your oven to 425°F (220°C). Line a baking sheet with parchment paper.
    - In a large bowl, toss the bell pepper, zucchini, cherry tomatoes, and red onion with olive oil, dried oregano, garlic powder, salt, and pepper.
    - Spread the vegetables in a single layer on the prepared baking sheet.
    - Roast for 20-25 minutes, or until the vegetables are tender and slightly caramelized, stirring halfway through.
2. **Prepare the Wraps:**
    - Warm the tortillas slightly in a dry skillet or microwave for about 10-15 seconds to make them more pliable.
    - Spread a generous layer of hummus on each tortilla.
    - Arrange the roasted vegetables over the hummus.
    - Top with baby spinach or arugula, crumbled feta cheese, and avocado slices if using.
3. **Wrap and Serve:**
    - Roll up each tortilla tightly, folding in the sides as you go to form a wrap.
    - Slice in half diagonally if desired.
    - Serve with lemon wedges on the side for a fresh squeeze of citrus, if you like.

Enjoy your tasty and healthy Roasted Veggie and Hummus Wrap!

Edamame and Corn Salad

Ingredients:

- **For the Salad:**
    - 1 cup frozen edamame (shelled)
    - 1 cup corn kernels (fresh, frozen, or canned, drained)
    - 1 red bell pepper, diced
    - 1/2 red onion, finely diced
    - 1 cup cherry tomatoes, halved
    - 1/4 cup fresh cilantro or parsley, chopped
- **For the Dressing:**
    - 3 tablespoons extra-virgin olive oil
    - 2 tablespoons lime juice (about 1 lime)
    - 1 tablespoon honey or maple syrup
    - 1 clove garlic, minced
    - 1/2 teaspoon ground cumin
    - Salt and pepper, to taste

Instructions:

1. **Cook the Edamame and Corn:**
    - For edamame, cook according to package instructions. If using frozen edamame, boil for about 3-5 minutes until tender, then drain and cool.
    - For corn, if using fresh or frozen, cook in boiling water for 2-3 minutes until tender, then drain and cool. If using canned corn, simply drain it.
2. **Prepare the Vegetables:**
    - In a large bowl, combine the cooked edamame, corn, diced red bell pepper, finely diced red onion, cherry tomatoes, and chopped cilantro or parsley.
3. **Make the Dressing:**
    - In a small bowl or jar, whisk together the olive oil, lime juice, honey or maple syrup, minced garlic, ground cumin, salt, and pepper until well combined.
4. **Combine and Serve:**
    - Pour the dressing over the salad and toss gently to coat all ingredients evenly.
    - Serve immediately or chill in the refrigerator for 30 minutes to allow the flavors to meld.

Enjoy your delicious and nutritious Edamame and Corn Salad!

Chickpea and Spinach Stuffed Pita

Ingredients:

- **For the Stuffing:**
    - 1 can (15 oz) chickpeas, drained and rinsed
    - 2 cups fresh spinach, chopped
    - 1 tablespoon olive oil
    - 1 clove garlic, minced
    - 1/2 teaspoon ground cumin
    - 1/2 teaspoon smoked paprika
    - 1/4 teaspoon ground turmeric (optional)
    - Salt and pepper, to taste
    - 1/4 cup crumbled feta cheese (optional)
    - 1 tablespoon fresh lemon juice
- **For Assembly:**
    - 4 whole wheat or regular pita breads
    - 1/2 cup plain Greek yogurt (optional, for serving)
    - 1/2 cucumber, sliced (optional, for serving)
    - Sliced cherry tomatoes (optional, for serving)

Instructions:

1. **Prepare the Chickpea and Spinach Filling:**
    - Heat olive oil in a large skillet over medium heat.
    - Add minced garlic and cook for 1 minute, until fragrant.
    - Add chickpeas to the skillet and cook for 3-4 minutes, stirring occasionally.
    - Stir in ground cumin, smoked paprika, turmeric (if using), salt, and pepper.
    - Add chopped spinach and cook for another 2-3 minutes, until the spinach is wilted and the chickpeas are heated through.
    - Remove from heat and stir in crumbled feta cheese and lemon juice if using. Mix well.
2. **Prepare the Pita:**
    - Warm the pita breads slightly in a dry skillet or microwave for about 10-15 seconds to make them more pliable.
3. **Assemble the Pitas:**
    - Carefully cut or open each pita bread to create a pocket.
    - Stuff each pita with the chickpea and spinach filling.
4. **Serve:**
    - Serve the stuffed pitas with a side of plain Greek yogurt, sliced cucumber, and cherry tomatoes if desired.

Enjoy your healthy and satisfying Chickpea and Spinach Stuffed Pita!

Turkey and Spinach Breakfast Casserole

Ingredients:

- **For the Casserole:**
    - 1 tablespoon olive oil
    - 1/2 pound ground turkey
    - 1 cup fresh spinach, chopped
    - 1/2 onion, diced
    - 1 bell pepper (any color), diced
    - 1 cup shredded cheese (cheddar, mozzarella, or your choice)
    - 6 large eggs
    - 1/2 cup milk (any type)
    - 1/2 teaspoon dried oregano
    - 1/2 teaspoon garlic powder
    - Salt and pepper, to taste

Instructions:

1. **Preheat the Oven:**
    - Preheat your oven to 375°F (190°C).
2. **Cook the Turkey and Vegetables:**
    - Heat olive oil in a large skillet over medium heat.
    - Add ground turkey and cook until browned and cooked through, breaking it up with a spoon.
    - Add diced onion and bell pepper, cooking for about 5 minutes until softened.
    - Stir in chopped spinach and cook for an additional 2-3 minutes, until wilted. Remove from heat.
3. **Prepare the Egg Mixture:**
    - In a large bowl, whisk together eggs, milk, dried oregano, garlic powder, salt, and pepper.
4. **Assemble the Casserole:**
    - Spread the turkey and vegetable mixture evenly in a greased 9x13-inch baking dish.
    - Sprinkle shredded cheese over the top of the turkey mixture.
    - Pour the egg mixture over the top, ensuring it covers all the ingredients.
5. **Bake:**
    - Bake in the preheated oven for 30-35 minutes, or until the eggs are set and the top is lightly golden.
6. **Cool and Serve:**
    - Allow the casserole to cool slightly before slicing into squares.

Enjoy your delicious Turkey and Spinach Breakfast Casserole!

Baked Salmon with Lemon and Dill

Ingredients:

- 4 salmon fillets (about 6 oz each)
- 2 tablespoons olive oil
- 1 lemon, thinly sliced
- 2 cloves garlic, minced
- 1 tablespoon fresh dill, chopped (or 1 teaspoon dried dill)
- Salt and pepper, to taste
- Lemon wedges (for serving)

Instructions:

1. **Preheat the Oven:**
   - Preheat your oven to 400°F (200°C). Line a baking sheet with parchment paper or lightly grease it.
2. **Prepare the Salmon:**
   - Place the salmon fillets on the prepared baking sheet, skin-side down if the skin is still on.
3. **Season the Salmon:**
   - Brush the fillets with olive oil.
   - Sprinkle minced garlic, chopped dill, salt, and pepper evenly over the salmon.
   - Arrange lemon slices on top of the fillets.
4. **Bake:**
   - Bake in the preheated oven for 12-15 minutes, or until the salmon flakes easily with a fork and reaches an internal temperature of 145°F (63°C).
5. **Serve:**
   - Remove from the oven and let rest for a few minutes.
   - Serve with additional lemon wedges if desired.

Enjoy your delicious and healthy Baked Salmon with Lemon and Dill!

Broccoli and Cheddar Stuffed Sweet Potatoes

Ingredients:

- **For the Sweet Potatoes:**
    - 4 medium sweet potatoes
    - 1 tablespoon olive oil
    - Salt and pepper, to taste
- **For the Broccoli and Cheddar Filling:**
    - 2 cups broccoli florets, chopped
    - 1 cup shredded cheddar cheese
    - 1 tablespoon olive oil
    - 2 cloves garlic, minced
    - 1/4 teaspoon dried thyme (optional)
    - Salt and pepper, to taste
- **For Garnish (optional):**
    - 2 tablespoons chopped fresh chives or green onions

Instructions:

1. **Preheat the Oven:**
    - Preheat your oven to 400°F (200°C). Line a baking sheet with parchment paper or lightly grease it.
2. **Prepare the Sweet Potatoes:**
    - Wash and scrub the sweet potatoes.
    - Prick each sweet potato a few times with a fork.
    - Rub the sweet potatoes with olive oil and season with salt and pepper.
    - Place on the baking sheet and bake for 40-50 minutes, or until tender when pierced with a fork.
3. **Prepare the Broccoli and Cheddar Filling:**
    - While the sweet potatoes are baking, heat olive oil in a skillet over medium heat.
    - Add minced garlic and cook for 1 minute, until fragrant.
    - Add the chopped broccoli and cook for about 5-7 minutes, until tender but still bright green. Season with salt, pepper, and dried thyme if using.
    - Stir in the shredded cheddar cheese until melted and well combined.
4. **Assemble the Stuffed Sweet Potatoes:**
    - Once the sweet potatoes are done, remove them from the oven and let cool slightly.
    - Slice each sweet potato down the center, gently fluffing the flesh with a fork.
    - Spoon the broccoli and cheddar mixture into each sweet potato.
5. **Serve:**
    - Garnish with chopped fresh chives or green onions if desired.
    - Serve warm.

Enjoy your nutritious and delicious Broccoli and Cheddar Stuffed Sweet Potatoes!

Avocado and Egg Breakfast Bowl

Ingredients:

- 1 ripe avocado
- 2 large eggs
- 1 tablespoon olive oil or butter
- 1/2 cup cherry tomatoes, halved
- 1/4 cup cooked quinoa or brown rice (optional, for added texture)
- 1 tablespoon fresh cilantro or parsley, chopped
- 1/2 teaspoon ground paprika or chili powder (optional)
- Salt and pepper, to taste
- Lemon wedge (optional, for serving)

Instructions:

1. **Prepare the Avocado:**
   - Cut the avocado in half, remove the pit, and scoop out the flesh. Dice or slice the avocado as preferred.
2. **Cook the Eggs:**
   - Heat olive oil or butter in a non-stick skillet over medium heat.
   - Crack the eggs into the skillet and cook to your desired doneness (fried, scrambled, or poached). For fried eggs, cook until the whites are set but the yolks are still runny, or longer if you prefer them cooked through.
3. **Assemble the Breakfast Bowl:**
   - In a bowl, start with a base of cooked quinoa or brown rice if using.
   - Arrange the diced or sliced avocado and cherry tomatoes on top.
   - Place the cooked eggs on top of the avocado and tomatoes.
4. **Season and Garnish:**
   - Season with salt, pepper, and ground paprika or chili powder if desired.
   - Sprinkle with chopped fresh cilantro or parsley.
   - Serve with a lemon wedge for a squeeze of fresh citrus, if desired.

Enjoy your healthy and satisfying Avocado and Egg Breakfast Bowl!

Spicy Black Bean and Sweet Potato Tacos

Ingredients:

- **For the Filling:**
    - 1 large sweet potato, peeled and diced
    - 1 can (15 oz) black beans, drained and rinsed
    - 1 tablespoon olive oil
    - 1 teaspoon smoked paprika
    - 1/2 teaspoon ground cumin
    - 1/2 teaspoon chili powder
    - 1/4 teaspoon cayenne pepper (optional, for extra heat)
    - Salt and pepper, to taste
    - 1 cup corn kernels (fresh, frozen, or canned)
- **For the Tacos:**
    - 8 small corn or flour tortillas
    - 1 avocado, sliced
    - 1/2 cup crumbled feta or shredded cheese (optional)
    - Fresh cilantro, chopped
    - Lime wedges (for serving)
    - Salsa or hot sauce (optional)

Instructions:

1. **Cook the Sweet Potatoes:**
    - Preheat your oven to 400°F (200°C). Line a baking sheet with parchment paper.
    - Toss the diced sweet potatoes with olive oil, smoked paprika, ground cumin, chili powder, cayenne pepper (if using), salt, and pepper.
    - Spread the sweet potatoes in a single layer on the baking sheet and roast for 20-25 minutes, or until tender and slightly caramelized.
2. **Prepare the Black Beans and Corn:**
    - In a skillet over medium heat, add the black beans and corn. Cook for 5 minutes, stirring occasionally, until heated through. Season with a little salt and pepper.
3. **Assemble the Tacos:**
    - Warm the tortillas in a dry skillet or microwave until pliable.
    - Fill each tortilla with a portion of roasted sweet potatoes, black beans, and corn.
4. **Garnish and Serve:**
    - Top with avocado slices, crumbled feta or shredded cheese if using, and fresh cilantro.
    - Serve with lime wedges and salsa or hot sauce on the side, if desired.

Enjoy your delicious and spicy Black Bean and Sweet Potato Tacos!

Sweet Potato and Avocado Breakfast Tacos

Ingredients:

- **For the Sweet Potatoes:**
    - 1 large sweet potato, peeled and diced
    - 1 tablespoon olive oil
    - 1/2 teaspoon ground cumin
    - 1/2 teaspoon smoked paprika
    - 1/4 teaspoon garlic powder
    - 1/4 teaspoon chili powder
    - Salt and pepper, to taste
- **For the Tacos:**
    - 8 small corn or flour tortillas
    - 1 ripe avocado, sliced
    - 1/2 cup crumbled feta or shredded cheese (optional)
    - 1/4 cup fresh cilantro, chopped
    - 1/4 cup diced red onion
    - 1/4 cup chopped fresh tomatoes or salsa
    - Lime wedges (for serving)

Instructions:

1. **Prepare the Sweet Potatoes:**
    - Preheat your oven to 400°F (200°C). Line a baking sheet with parchment paper.
    - Toss the diced sweet potatoes with olive oil, ground cumin, smoked paprika, garlic powder, chili powder, salt, and pepper.
    - Spread the sweet potatoes in a single layer on the baking sheet.
    - Roast for 20-25 minutes, or until tender and slightly caramelized, stirring halfway through.
2. **Warm the Tortillas:**
    - Warm the tortillas in a dry skillet over medium heat for about 30 seconds per side, or wrap in a damp paper towel and microwave for 20-30 seconds until warm and pliable.
3. **Assemble the Tacos:**
    - Divide the roasted sweet potatoes evenly among the tortillas.
    - Top each taco with avocado slices, crumbled feta or shredded cheese if using, diced red onion, and chopped tomatoes or salsa.
    - Sprinkle with fresh cilantro.
4. **Serve:**
    - Serve the tacos with lime wedges on the side for a squeeze of fresh lime juice.

Enjoy your vibrant and flavorful Sweet Potato and Avocado Breakfast Tacos!

Fresh Fruit Salad with Mint

Ingredients:

- **For the Fruit Salad:**
    - 1 cup strawberries, hulled and sliced
    - 1 cup blueberries
    - 1 cup grapes, halved
    - 1 orange, peeled and segmented
    - 1 kiwi, peeled and sliced
    - 1 cup cubed pineapple
    - 1 banana, sliced (optional, to add just before serving)
- **For the Mint Dressing:**
    - 2 tablespoons honey or maple syrup
    - 2 tablespoons fresh lime juice
    - 2 tablespoons fresh mint leaves, finely chopped

Instructions:

1. **Prepare the Fruit:**
    - In a large bowl, combine the strawberries, blueberries, grapes, orange segments, kiwi, and pineapple. If using, add the banana just before serving to prevent browning.
2. **Make the Mint Dressing:**
    - In a small bowl or jar, whisk together the honey or maple syrup, lime juice, and chopped mint leaves.
3. **Combine and Serve:**
    - Pour the mint dressing over the fruit salad.
    - Gently toss to coat the fruit evenly with the dressing.
    - Chill in the refrigerator for at least 30 minutes before serving to allow the flavors to meld.

Enjoy your refreshing Fresh Fruit Salad with Mint!

Almond Flour Muffins with Blueberries

Ingredients:

- **For the Muffins:**
    - 2 cups almond flour
    - 1/2 teaspoon baking soda
    - 1/4 teaspoon salt
    - 3 large eggs
    - 1/4 cup honey or maple syrup
    - 1/4 cup coconut oil or butter, melted
    - 1 teaspoon vanilla extract
    - 1 cup fresh or frozen blueberries
- **Optional Topping:**
    - 1 tablespoon almond flour
    - 1 tablespoon honey or maple syrup
    - 1/4 teaspoon ground cinnamon

Instructions:

1. **Preheat the Oven:**
    - Preheat your oven to 350°F (175°C). Line a 12-cup muffin tin with paper liners or grease the tin with non-stick spray.
2. **Prepare the Muffin Batter:**
    - In a large bowl, whisk together almond flour, baking soda, and salt.
    - In another bowl, whisk together the eggs, honey or maple syrup, melted coconut oil or butter, and vanilla extract until well combined.
    - Pour the wet ingredients into the dry ingredients and stir until just combined.
    - Gently fold in the blueberries.
3. **Fill the Muffin Tin:**
    - Divide the batter evenly among the muffin cups, filling each about 3/4 full.
4. **Add Optional Topping:**
    - In a small bowl, mix 1 tablespoon almond flour with 1 tablespoon honey or maple syrup and 1/4 teaspoon ground cinnamon.
    - Sprinkle this mixture over the top of the muffin batter in each cup for added texture and sweetness.
5. **Bake:**
    - Bake in the preheated oven for 20-25 minutes, or until the muffins are golden brown and a toothpick inserted into the center comes out clean.
6. **Cool and Serve:**
    - Allow the muffins to cool in the tin for 5 minutes before transferring to a wire rack to cool completely.

Enjoy your Almond Flour Muffins with Blueberries!

Veggie-Packed Quiche with a Sweet Potato Crust

Ingredients:

- **For the Sweet Potato Crust:**
    - 2 large sweet potatoes, peeled and grated
    - 1 tablespoon olive oil
    - 1/2 teaspoon salt
    - 1/4 teaspoon black pepper
    - 1/4 teaspoon paprika
- **For the Quiche Filling:**
    - 1 tablespoon olive oil
    - 1/2 cup onion, diced
    - 1 bell pepper, diced
    - 1 cup spinach, chopped
    - 1 cup mushrooms, sliced
    - 1 cup shredded cheese (cheddar, mozzarella, or your choice)
    - 4 large eggs
    - 1/2 cup milk (any type)
    - 1/4 teaspoon dried thyme
    - 1/4 teaspoon dried basil
    - Salt and pepper, to taste

Instructions:

1. **Prepare the Sweet Potato Crust:**
    - Preheat your oven to 375°F (190°C). Grease a 9-inch pie dish or quiche pan.
    - In a large bowl, mix the grated sweet potatoes with olive oil, salt, pepper, and paprika.
    - Press the sweet potato mixture into the bottom and up the sides of the prepared pie dish to form an even crust.
    - Bake the crust for 20 minutes, then remove from the oven and let cool slightly.
2. **Prepare the Quiche Filling:**
    - While the crust is baking, heat olive oil in a skillet over medium heat.
    - Add the onion and bell pepper and cook for 5 minutes, until softened.
    - Add the mushrooms and cook for an additional 3-4 minutes.
    - Stir in the spinach and cook until wilted. Remove from heat and let cool slightly.
3. **Assemble the Quiche:**
    - In a bowl, whisk together the eggs, milk, dried thyme, dried basil, salt, and pepper.
    - Spread the cooked vegetable mixture evenly over the pre-baked sweet potato crust.
    - Sprinkle shredded cheese over the vegetables.

- Pour the egg mixture over the top, making sure it evenly covers the vegetables and cheese.
4. **Bake the Quiche:**
    - Bake in the preheated oven for 30-35 minutes, or until the quiche is set and the top is golden brown.
5. **Cool and Serve:**
    - Let the quiche cool for a few minutes before slicing.

Enjoy your Veggie-Packed Quiche with a Sweet Potato Crust!

Greek Salad with Chicken

Ingredients:

- **For the Salad:**
    - 2 cups cooked chicken breast, diced (grilled or rotisserie chicken works well)
    - 4 cups mixed greens (e.g., romaine, spinach, arugula)
    - 1 cucumber, sliced
    - 1 cup cherry tomatoes, halved
    - 1/2 red onion, thinly sliced
    - 1/2 cup Kalamata olives, pitted
    - 1/2 cup feta cheese, crumbled
    - 1/4 cup sliced pepperoncini (optional)
- **For the Dressing:**
    - 1/4 cup extra-virgin olive oil
    - 2 tablespoons red wine vinegar
    - 1 teaspoon Dijon mustard
    - 1 teaspoon dried oregano
    - 1 clove garlic, minced
    - Salt and pepper, to taste

Instructions:

1. **Prepare the Chicken:**
    - If not already cooked, season the chicken breasts with salt, pepper, and a bit of olive oil. Grill or bake until cooked through and juices run clear, about 6-8 minutes per side, depending on thickness. Allow to cool slightly, then dice.
2. **Prepare the Salad Ingredients:**
    - In a large bowl, combine mixed greens, cucumber, cherry tomatoes, red onion, Kalamata olives, and feta cheese. Add pepperoncini if using.
3. **Make the Dressing:**
    - In a small bowl or jar, whisk together olive oil, red wine vinegar, Dijon mustard, dried oregano, minced garlic, salt, and pepper until well combined.
4. **Assemble the Salad:**
    - Add the diced chicken to the salad ingredients and toss gently to combine.
    - Drizzle the dressing over the salad and toss again to coat everything evenly.
5. **Serve:**
    - Serve immediately, or chill the salad in the refrigerator for about 30 minutes to let the flavors meld.

Enjoy your Greek Salad with Chicken!

Tofu and Veggie Stir-Fry

Ingredients:

- **For the Stir-Fry:**
    - 1 block (14 oz) firm tofu, drained and cubed
    - 2 tablespoons vegetable oil
    - 1 bell pepper, sliced
    - 1 cup broccoli florets
    - 1 cup snap peas or snow peas
    - 1 cup carrots, sliced
    - 2 cloves garlic, minced
    - 1 tablespoon fresh ginger, minced
    - 2 green onions, sliced
- **For the Sauce:**
    - 1/4 cup soy sauce or tamari
    - 2 tablespoons hoisin sauce
    - 1 tablespoon rice vinegar
    - 1 tablespoon sesame oil
    - 1 teaspoon cornstarch mixed with 1 tablespoon water (optional, for thickening)

Instructions:

1. **Prepare the Tofu:**
    - Heat 1 tablespoon of vegetable oil in a large skillet or wok over medium-high heat.
    - Add the tofu cubes and cook until golden and crispy on all sides, about 8-10 minutes. Remove tofu from the skillet and set aside.
2. **Cook the Vegetables:**
    - In the same skillet, add the remaining 1 tablespoon of vegetable oil.
    - Add the garlic and ginger, and sauté for 1 minute until fragrant.
    - Add bell pepper, broccoli, snap peas, and carrots. Stir-fry for 4-5 minutes, or until vegetables are tender-crisp.
3. **Add the Tofu and Sauce:**
    - Return the tofu to the skillet with the vegetables.
    - In a small bowl, whisk together soy sauce, hoisin sauce, rice vinegar, and sesame oil. Pour over the tofu and vegetables.
    - Stir well to coat everything evenly. If you want a thicker sauce, stir in the cornstarch mixture and cook for an additional 1-2 minutes until the sauce thickens.
4. **Serve:**
    - Garnish with sliced green onions and serve over cooked rice or noodles.

Enjoy your delicious Tofu and Veggie Stir-Fry!

Baked Apples with Cinnamon and Walnuts

Ingredients:

- 4 large apples (such as Honeycrisp or Granny Smith)
- 1/4 cup walnuts, chopped
- 1/4 cup raisins or dried cranberries (optional)
- 2 tablespoons honey or maple syrup
- 1 teaspoon ground cinnamon
- 1/4 teaspoon ground nutmeg (optional)
- 1 tablespoon butter (optional, for extra richness)
- Vanilla ice cream or yogurt (optional, for serving)

Instructions:

1. **Preheat the Oven:**
   - Preheat your oven to 350°F (175°C). Grease a baking dish.
2. **Prepare the Apples:**
   - Core the apples, making a hollow center but leaving the bottom intact to hold the filling.
3. **Make the Filling:**
   - In a small bowl, mix together the chopped walnuts, raisins or dried cranberries, honey or maple syrup, ground cinnamon, and nutmeg if using.
4. **Stuff the Apples:**
   - Fill each apple with the walnut mixture, packing it in gently.
5. **Bake:**
   - Place the stuffed apples in the prepared baking dish. Dot each apple with a small piece of butter if using.
   - Bake in the preheated oven for 20-25 minutes, or until the apples are tender but still hold their shape.
6. **Serve:**
   - Let the apples cool slightly before serving.
   - Serve warm with a scoop of vanilla ice cream or a dollop of yogurt if desired.

Enjoy your delicious Baked Apples with Cinnamon and Walnuts!

Protein-Packed Breakfast Smoothie with Spinach

Ingredients:

- 1 cup fresh spinach
- 1 banana, sliced
- 1/2 cup Greek yogurt (plain or vanilla)
- 1 scoop protein powder (vanilla or unflavored)
- 1/2 cup almond milk or any milk of your choice
- 1 tablespoon almond butter or peanut butter
- 1 tablespoon chia seeds (optional, for extra fiber and omega-3s)
- 1/2 cup frozen berries (e.g., blueberries, strawberries)
- 1 teaspoon honey or maple syrup (optional, for added sweetness)

Instructions:

1. **Blend Ingredients:**
    - In a blender, combine the spinach, banana, Greek yogurt, protein powder, almond milk, almond butter, chia seeds (if using), and frozen berries.
2. **Blend Until Smooth:**
    - Blend on high until the mixture is smooth and creamy. If the smoothie is too thick, add a little more almond milk to reach your desired consistency.
3. **Sweeten if Desired:**
    - Taste the smoothie and add honey or maple syrup if you prefer it sweeter. Blend again briefly to combine.
4. **Serve:**
    - Pour into a glass and enjoy immediately.

This smoothie is packed with protein, fiber, and vitamins to start your day off right!

Roasted Veggie and Hummus Wrap

Ingredients:

- **For the Roasted Veggies:**
    - 1 red bell pepper, sliced
    - 1 zucchini, sliced
    - 1 cup cherry tomatoes, halved
    - 1 red onion, sliced
    - 2 tablespoons olive oil
    - 1/2 teaspoon dried oregano
    - 1/2 teaspoon garlic powder
    - Salt and pepper, to taste
- **For the Wrap:**
    - 4 large whole wheat or flour tortillas
    - 1/2 cup hummus (any flavor)
    - 1 cup fresh spinach or mixed greens
    - 1/4 cup crumbled feta cheese (optional)
    - 1/4 cup sliced black olives (optional)

Instructions:

1. **Roast the Vegetables:**
    - Preheat your oven to 425°F (220°C). Line a baking sheet with parchment paper.
    - Toss the bell pepper, zucchini, cherry tomatoes, and red onion with olive oil, dried oregano, garlic powder, salt, and pepper.
    - Spread the vegetables in a single layer on the baking sheet and roast for 20-25 minutes, or until tender and slightly caramelized, stirring halfway through.
2. **Prepare the Wraps:**
    - While the veggies are roasting, warm the tortillas in a dry skillet over medium heat or in the microwave.
3. **Assemble the Wraps:**
    - Spread a layer of hummus over each tortilla.
    - Top with roasted vegetables, fresh spinach or mixed greens, crumbled feta cheese, and sliced black olives if using.
    - Roll up the tortillas tightly, folding in the sides as you go to enclose the filling.
4. **Serve:**
    - Slice the wraps in half and serve immediately, or wrap in foil for a portable meal.

Enjoy your Roasted Veggie and Hummus Wraps!

Sweet Potato Hash with Poached Eggs

Ingredients:

- **For the Hash:**
    - 2 large sweet potatoes, peeled and diced
    - 1 red bell pepper, diced
    - 1 small onion, diced
    - 1 cup baby spinach or kale
    - 2 tablespoons olive oil
    - 1 teaspoon paprika
    - 1/2 teaspoon garlic powder
    - 1/2 teaspoon ground cumin
    - Salt and pepper, to taste
- **For the Poached Eggs:**
    - 4 large eggs
    - 1 tablespoon vinegar (optional, helps with poaching)
    - Water (for poaching)

Instructions:

1. **Prepare the Sweet Potato Hash:**
    - Heat olive oil in a large skillet over medium heat.
    - Add the diced sweet potatoes and cook for about 10 minutes, stirring occasionally, until they begin to soften.
    - Add the diced red bell pepper and onion. Continue to cook for another 10 minutes, stirring occasionally, until the sweet potatoes are tender and lightly browned.
    - Stir in the paprika, garlic powder, cumin, salt, and pepper.
    - Add the spinach or kale and cook for 1-2 minutes until wilted.
2. **Poach the Eggs:**
    - Fill a large saucepan with about 2 inches of water and bring to a gentle simmer. Add vinegar if using.
    - Crack each egg into a small bowl or ramekin.
    - Gently slide the eggs into the simmering water, one at a time. Cook for about 3-4 minutes for soft yolks or longer if you prefer them firmer.
    - Use a slotted spoon to remove the eggs and set aside on a paper towel to drain.
3. **Assemble and Serve:**
    - Divide the sweet potato hash among plates.
    - Top each serving with a poached egg.
    - Season with additional salt and pepper, and garnish with fresh herbs if desired.

Enjoy your Sweet Potato Hash with Poached Eggs!

Chia Seed Pudding with Almond Milk

Ingredients:

- 1/4 cup chia seeds
- 1 cup unsweetened almond milk (or any milk of your choice)
- 1-2 tablespoons maple syrup or honey (to taste)
- 1/2 teaspoon vanilla extract (optional)
- **Toppings (optional):**
    - Fresh fruit (berries, sliced banana, etc.)
    - Nuts or seeds
    - Granola
    - A drizzle of honey or maple syrup

Instructions:

1. **Mix the Pudding:**
    - In a bowl or jar, combine chia seeds, almond milk, maple syrup or honey, and vanilla extract if using.
    - Stir well to mix, ensuring that the chia seeds are evenly distributed and not clumped together.
2. **Refrigerate:**
    - Cover the bowl or jar and refrigerate for at least 4 hours, or overnight. The chia seeds will absorb the liquid and the mixture will thicken into a pudding-like consistency.
3. **Serve:**
    - Stir the pudding before serving. If it's too thick, you can add a little more almond milk to reach your desired consistency.
    - Top with fresh fruit, nuts, granola, or a drizzle of honey or maple syrup.

Enjoy your creamy and nutritious Chia Seed Pudding with Almond Milk!

Whole Wheat Banana Pancakes

Ingredients:

- **For the Pancakes:**
    - 1 cup whole wheat flour
    - 1 tablespoon baking powder
    - 1/2 teaspoon salt
    - 1 cup milk (any type; dairy or plant-based)
    - 2 ripe bananas, mashed
    - 1 large egg
    - 2 tablespoons honey or maple syrup
    - 2 tablespoons melted coconut oil or butter
    - 1/2 teaspoon vanilla extract (optional)
- **For Cooking:**
    - Cooking spray or additional butter for greasing the pan

Instructions:

1. **Prepare the Dry Ingredients:**
    - In a large bowl, whisk together the whole wheat flour, baking powder, and salt.
2. **Prepare the Wet Ingredients:**
    - In another bowl, combine the milk, mashed bananas, egg, honey or maple syrup, melted coconut oil or butter, and vanilla extract if using.
3. **Combine Ingredients:**
    - Pour the wet ingredients into the dry ingredients. Stir gently until just combined. The batter will be a bit lumpy, which is fine. Avoid over-mixing.
4. **Heat the Pan:**
    - Heat a non-stick skillet or griddle over medium heat. Lightly grease with cooking spray or a small amount of butter.
5. **Cook the Pancakes:**
    - Pour 1/4 cup of batter onto the skillet for each pancake. Cook until bubbles form on the surface and the edges look set, about 2-3 minutes.
    - Flip the pancake and cook for another 1-2 minutes, or until golden brown and cooked through.
6. **Serve:**
    - Keep the pancakes warm in a low oven while you cook the remaining pancakes, or serve immediately with your favorite toppings.

Topping Ideas:

- Fresh fruit (berries, banana slices, etc.)
- Maple syrup or honey
- Greek yogurt or nut butter

- Nuts or seeds

Enjoy your nutritious Whole Wheat Banana Pancakes!

Green Smoothie with Spinach and Apple

Ingredients:

- 1 cup fresh spinach leaves
- 1 apple, cored and chopped (leave the skin on for extra fiber)
- 1/2 banana (for creaminess)
- 1/2 cup Greek yogurt or a plant-based yogurt (optional, for added creaminess)
- 1/2 cup almond milk or any milk of your choice
- 1 tablespoon chia seeds or flaxseeds (optional, for extra nutrients)
- 1/2 teaspoon honey or maple syrup (optional, for sweetness)
- 1/2 cup ice (optional, for a colder smoothie)

Instructions:

1. **Blend Ingredients:**
   - Add spinach, apple, banana, Greek yogurt (if using), almond milk, and chia seeds or flaxseeds (if using) to a blender.
2. **Sweeten if Desired:**
   - Blend until smooth. Taste and add honey or maple syrup if you prefer a sweeter smoothie.
3. **Adjust Consistency:**
   - Add ice if you want a colder, thicker smoothie and blend again until smooth.
4. **Serve:**
   - Pour into a glass and enjoy immediately.

This green smoothie is packed with nutrients and perfect for a quick, healthy snack or breakfast!

Berry and Spinach Smoothie Bowl

Ingredients:

- **For the Smoothie Base:**
    - 1 cup fresh spinach leaves
    - 1 cup mixed berries (such as strawberries, blueberries, raspberries, or blackberries; fresh or frozen)
    - 1/2 banana (for creaminess)
    - 1/2 cup Greek yogurt or a plant-based yogurt (optional, for added creaminess)
    - 1/2 cup almond milk or any milk of your choice
    - 1 tablespoon chia seeds or flaxseeds (optional, for extra nutrients)
    - 1 tablespoon honey or maple syrup (optional, for sweetness)
- **For Toppings:**
    - Fresh berries (strawberries, blueberries, raspberries, etc.)
    - Sliced banana
    - Granola
    - Nuts or seeds (e.g., almonds, chia seeds)
    - Coconut flakes
    - A drizzle of honey or maple syrup (optional)

Instructions:

1. **Prepare the Smoothie Base:**
    - In a blender, combine the spinach, mixed berries, banana, Greek yogurt (if using), and almond milk. Blend until smooth. If the mixture is too thick, add a little more almond milk to reach your desired consistency.
2. **Sweeten if Desired:**
    - Taste the smoothie base and add honey or maple syrup if you prefer additional sweetness. Blend briefly to combine.
3. **Assemble the Smoothie Bowl:**
    - Pour the smoothie base into a bowl.
4. **Add Toppings:**
    - Decorate the top of the smoothie with fresh berries, sliced banana, granola, nuts or seeds, and coconut flakes. Drizzle with honey or maple syrup if desired.
5. **Serve:**
    - Enjoy immediately with a spoon!

This Berry and Spinach Smoothie Bowl is not only delicious but also packed with vitamins, minerals, and antioxidants. It makes for a great breakfast or a nutritious snack.

Cottage Cheese with Pineapple and Almonds

Ingredients:

- 1 cup cottage cheese (low-fat or full-fat, based on your preference)
- 1/2 cup fresh pineapple chunks (or canned pineapple, drained)
- 2 tablespoons sliced almonds (toasted or raw)
- 1 tablespoon honey or maple syrup (optional, for added sweetness)
- A sprinkle of cinnamon (optional, for extra flavor)

Instructions:

1. **Prepare the Ingredients:**
    - If using fresh pineapple, peel and cut it into chunks. If using canned pineapple, ensure it's well-drained to avoid excess moisture.
2. **Assemble the Dish:**
    - In a bowl, combine the cottage cheese and pineapple chunks.
3. **Add Toppings:**
    - Sprinkle sliced almonds on top of the cottage cheese and pineapple mixture.
    - Drizzle with honey or maple syrup if you like a touch of sweetness.
    - Add a sprinkle of cinnamon if desired.
4. **Serve:**
    - Enjoy immediately as a quick snack or a light breakfast.

This Cottage Cheese with Pineapple and Almonds is a perfect blend of creamy, sweet, and crunchy, providing a great balance of protein, fruit, and healthy fats.

Kale and Mushroom Frittata
Ingredients:

1 tablespoon olive oil
1 cup mushrooms, sliced
2 cups fresh kale, chopped
1 small onion, diced
6 large eggs
1/4 cup milk (any type; dairy or plant-based)
1/2 cup shredded cheese (optional; e.g., cheddar, feta, or mozzarella)
Salt and pepper, to taste
1/4 teaspoon garlic powder (optional)
Instructions:

Preheat the Oven:

Preheat your oven to 375°F (190°C).
Cook the Vegetables:

Heat olive oil in a skillet over medium heat.
Add the diced onion and cook until softened, about 3-4 minutes.
Add the sliced mushrooms and cook until they release their moisture and start to brown, about 5 minutes.
Add the chopped kale and cook until wilted, about 2 minutes. Season with salt, pepper, and garlic powder if using.
Prepare the Egg Mixture:

In a bowl, whisk together the eggs, milk, and half of the shredded cheese (if using). Season with salt and pepper.
Combine and Cook:

Pour the egg mixture over the cooked vegetables in the skillet. Stir gently to distribute the vegetables evenly.
Sprinkle the remaining cheese on top.
Bake the Frittata:

Transfer the skillet to the preheated oven.
Bake for 15-20 minutes, or until the frittata is set and the top is lightly golden.
Serve:

Let the frittata cool slightly before slicing. Serve warm or at room temperature.
Enjoy your Kale and Mushroom Frittata for a healthy and satisfying meal!

Almond Butter and Banana Smoothie

Ingredients:

- 1 ripe banana
- 2 tablespoons almond butter
- 1 cup milk (any type; dairy or plant-based)
- 1/2 cup Greek yogurt or a plant-based yogurt (optional, for extra creaminess)
- 1 tablespoon honey or maple syrup (optional, for added sweetness)
- 1/2 teaspoon vanilla extract (optional, for extra flavor)
- 1/4 teaspoon ground cinnamon (optional, for a touch of spice)
- 1/2 cup ice (optional, for a colder smoothie)

Instructions:

1. **Blend Ingredients:**
    - In a blender, combine the banana, almond butter, milk, Greek yogurt (if using), honey or maple syrup (if using), vanilla extract (if using), and ground cinnamon (if using).
2. **Adjust Consistency:**
    - Blend until smooth. If the smoothie is too thick, add a bit more milk to reach your desired consistency. For a colder smoothie, add ice and blend again until smooth.
3. **Serve:**
    - Pour into a glass and enjoy immediately.

This Almond Butter and Banana Smoothie is packed with protein, healthy fats, and delicious flavor, making it a perfect choice for a quick breakfast or a satisfying snack!

Whole Grain French Toast with Fresh Berries

Ingredients:

- **For the French Toast:**
    - 4 slices whole grain bread
    - 2 large eggs
    - 1/2 cup milk (any type; dairy or plant-based)
    - 1/2 teaspoon vanilla extract
    - 1/2 teaspoon ground cinnamon
    - 1 tablespoon honey or maple syrup (optional, for added sweetness)
    - Butter or oil for cooking
- **For the Toppings:**
    - 1 cup fresh berries (e.g., strawberries, blueberries, raspberries)
    - 2 tablespoons maple syrup or honey (optional, for drizzling)
    - Powdered sugar (optional, for dusting)

Instructions:

1. **Prepare the Egg Mixture:**
    - In a shallow dish, whisk together the eggs, milk, vanilla extract, ground cinnamon, and honey or maple syrup if using.
2. **Heat the Pan:**
    - Heat a skillet or griddle over medium heat and lightly grease with butter or oil.
3. **Cook the French Toast:**
    - Dip each slice of whole grain bread into the egg mixture, coating both sides.
    - Cook the bread slices in the skillet for 2-3 minutes per side, or until golden brown and cooked through.
4. **Prepare the Toppings:**
    - While the French toast is cooking, wash and prepare the fresh berries.
5. **Serve:**
    - Place the cooked French toast on plates. Top with fresh berries.
    - Drizzle with maple syrup or honey if desired, and dust with powdered sugar if using.

Enjoy your wholesome Whole Grain French Toast with Fresh Berries!

Apple and Walnut Oat Muffins

Ingredients:

- **Dry Ingredients:**
    - 1 cup rolled oats
    - 1 cup whole wheat flour
    - 1/2 cup chopped walnuts
    - 1/2 cup brown sugar or coconut sugar
    - 1 teaspoon baking powder
    - 1/2 teaspoon baking soda
    - 1/2 teaspoon ground cinnamon
    - 1/4 teaspoon salt
- **Wet Ingredients:**
    - 1/2 cup unsweetened applesauce
    - 1/2 cup milk (any type; dairy or plant-based)
    - 1/4 cup vegetable oil or melted coconut oil
    - 2 large eggs
    - 1 teaspoon vanilla extract
    - 1 large apple, peeled, cored, and diced

Instructions:

1. **Preheat Oven:**
    - Preheat your oven to 350°F (175°C). Line a muffin tin with paper liners or lightly grease it.
2. **Combine Dry Ingredients:**
    - In a large bowl, mix together the oats, whole wheat flour, chopped walnuts, brown sugar, baking powder, baking soda, cinnamon, and salt.
3. **Combine Wet Ingredients:**
    - In another bowl, whisk together the applesauce, milk, oil, eggs, and vanilla extract.
4. **Mix Ingredients:**
    - Add the wet ingredients to the dry ingredients and stir until just combined. Gently fold in the diced apple.
5. **Fill Muffin Tin:**
    - Divide the batter evenly among the muffin cups, filling each about 2/3 full.
6. **Bake:**
    - Bake for 20-25 minutes, or until a toothpick inserted into the center of a muffin comes out clean.
7. **Cool:**
    - Allow the muffins to cool in the pan for a few minutes before transferring them to a wire rack to cool completely.

Enjoy your Apple and Walnut Oat Muffins as a delicious and nutritious snack or breakfast!

Spicy Black Bean and Sweet Potato Tacos

Ingredients:

- **For the Filling:**
    - 1 large sweet potato, peeled and diced
    - 1 tablespoon olive oil
    - 1 teaspoon chili powder
    - 1/2 teaspoon cumin
    - 1/2 teaspoon paprika
    - 1/4 teaspoon cayenne pepper (optional, for extra heat)
    - Salt and pepper, to taste
    - 1 can (15 oz) black beans, drained and rinsed
    - 1/2 cup corn kernels (fresh or frozen)
    - 1/2 cup diced red bell pepper
    - 1/2 cup diced red onion
- **For Serving:**
    - 8 small tortillas (corn or flour)
    - 1 avocado, sliced
    - 1 cup shredded lettuce or cabbage
    - 1/2 cup crumbled feta or shredded cheese (optional)
    - Fresh cilantro, chopped (for garnish)
    - Lime wedges (for serving)
    - Salsa or hot sauce (optional)

Instructions:

1. **Roast the Sweet Potatoes:**
    - Preheat your oven to 425°F (220°C). Toss the diced sweet potato with olive oil, chili powder, cumin, paprika, cayenne pepper (if using), salt, and pepper.
    - Spread the sweet potatoes on a baking sheet in a single layer. Roast for 20-25 minutes, or until tender and lightly caramelized, stirring halfway through.
2. **Prepare the Filling:**
    - In a skillet, heat a small amount of olive oil over medium heat. Add the diced red bell pepper and red onion, and cook until softened, about 5 minutes.
    - Stir in the black beans and corn, and cook until heated through. Season with salt and pepper to taste.
3. **Warm the Tortillas:**
    - Warm the tortillas in a dry skillet or microwave them until pliable.
4. **Assemble the Tacos:**
    - Divide the roasted sweet potatoes and black bean mixture among the tortillas.
    - Top with avocado slices, shredded lettuce or cabbage, crumbled feta or cheese (if using), and chopped cilantro.
5. **Serve:**

- Serve with lime wedges and your favorite salsa or hot sauce on the side.

Enjoy your Spicy Black Bean and Sweet Potato Tacos!

Veggie-Stuffed Omelette

Ingredients:

- **For the Omelette:**
    - 3 large eggs
    - 1 tablespoon milk or water
    - Salt and pepper, to taste
    - 1 tablespoon olive oil or butter
    - 1/4 cup diced onion
    - 1/4 cup diced bell pepper (any color)
    - 1/4 cup chopped spinach or kale
    - 1/4 cup cherry tomatoes, halved
    - 1/4 cup shredded cheese (optional; e.g., cheddar, feta, or mozzarella)
    - Fresh herbs (optional; e.g., chives, parsley, or basil), chopped for garnish

Instructions:

1. **Prepare the Vegetables:**
    - Heat the olive oil or butter in a non-stick skillet over medium heat.
    - Add the diced onion and cook for about 2-3 minutes, until softened.
    - Add the diced bell pepper and cook for another 2 minutes.
    - Stir in the spinach or kale and cook until wilted.
    - Add the cherry tomatoes and cook for an additional minute. Season with salt and pepper. Remove the vegetables from the skillet and set aside.
2. **Prepare the Egg Mixture:**
    - In a bowl, whisk together the eggs, milk or water, salt, and pepper.
3. **Cook the Omelette:**
    - In the same skillet, add a little more olive oil or butter if needed and heat over medium-low heat.
    - Pour the egg mixture into the skillet, tilting the pan to spread it evenly.
    - Let the eggs cook undisturbed for about 1-2 minutes, until the edges start to set.
4. **Add the Filling:**
    - Once the eggs are mostly set but still slightly runny on top, spoon the cooked vegetables evenly over one half of the omelette.
    - If using cheese, sprinkle it over the vegetables.
5. **Fold and Finish:**
    - Carefully fold the other half of the omelette over the filling.
    - Cook for an additional 1-2 minutes, until the cheese is melted (if using) and the omelette is cooked through.
6. **Serve:**
    - Slide the omelette onto a plate and garnish with fresh herbs if desired.

Enjoy your Veggie-Stuffed Omelette as a wholesome and satisfying breakfast or light meal!

Baked Eggplant with Tomato and Basil

Ingredients:

- 1 large eggplant, sliced into 1/2-inch rounds
- 2 tablespoons olive oil
- Salt and pepper, to taste
- 1 cup cherry tomatoes, halved (or 1 can of diced tomatoes, drained)
- 2 cloves garlic, minced
- 1/2 teaspoon dried oregano (optional)
- 1/4 cup fresh basil leaves, chopped (plus extra for garnish)
- 1/4 cup grated Parmesan cheese (optional)

Instructions:

1. **Preheat Oven:**
    - Preheat your oven to 400°F (200°C).
2. **Prepare the Eggplant:**
    - Arrange the eggplant slices on a baking sheet. Brush both sides with olive oil and season with salt and pepper.
3. **Bake the Eggplant:**
    - Bake in the preheated oven for 20 minutes, flipping halfway through, until the eggplant is tender and lightly browned.
4. **Prepare the Tomato Mixture:**
    - While the eggplant is baking, heat a small amount of olive oil in a pan over medium heat. Add the minced garlic and cook for about 1 minute until fragrant.
    - Add the cherry tomatoes (or diced tomatoes) and dried oregano if using. Cook for 5-7 minutes, until the tomatoes are softened and have released their juices. Stir in the fresh basil.
5. **Assemble the Dish:**
    - Once the eggplant is done baking, remove it from the oven. Spoon the tomato mixture evenly over the eggplant slices.
    - If using Parmesan cheese, sprinkle it over the top.
6. **Bake Again:**
    - Return the eggplant to the oven and bake for an additional 5-7 minutes, until the cheese is melted and bubbly (if using).
7. **Serve:**
    - Garnish with additional fresh basil leaves before serving.

Enjoy your Baked Eggplant with Tomato and Basil as a flavorful side dish or light main course!

Avocado Toast with Cherry Tomatoes

Ingredients:

- 2 slices whole-grain bread
- 1 ripe avocado
- 1 tablespoon lemon juice
- Salt and pepper, to taste
- 1/2 teaspoon red pepper flakes (optional, for a bit of heat)
- 1/2 cup cherry tomatoes, halved
- 1 tablespoon olive oil (optional)
- Fresh basil or parsley, chopped (for garnish, optional)

Instructions:

1. **Toast the Bread:**
    - Toast the whole-grain bread slices until they are golden brown and crispy.
2. **Prepare the Avocado:**
    - While the bread is toasting, cut the avocado in half, remove the pit, and scoop the flesh into a bowl.
    - Mash the avocado with a fork until smooth but still a bit chunky.
    - Stir in the lemon juice, and season with salt and pepper to taste. Add red pepper flakes if using.
3. **Prepare the Cherry Tomatoes:**
    - In a small bowl, toss the halved cherry tomatoes with a little olive oil if desired, and a pinch of salt and pepper.
4. **Assemble the Toast:**
    - Spread the mashed avocado evenly over the toasted bread slices.
    - Top with the halved cherry tomatoes.
5. **Garnish and Serve:**
    - Garnish with fresh basil or parsley if you like.
    - Serve immediately for the best texture and flavor.

This Avocado Toast with Cherry Tomatoes is perfect for a quick breakfast, snack, or light lunch, offering a balance of creamy avocado and juicy tomatoes with a hint of freshness and spice. Enjoy!

Cauliflower Rice Stir-Fry with Eggs

Ingredients:

- 1 medium head of cauliflower, riced (or 4 cups pre-riced cauliflower)
- 2 tablespoons olive oil or sesame oil
- 1 small onion, diced
- 2 cloves garlic, minced
- 1 cup mixed vegetables (e.g., bell peppers, carrots, peas, corn; fresh or frozen)
- 2 large eggs, beaten
- 3 tablespoons low-sodium soy sauce or tamari
- 1 tablespoon hoisin sauce (optional, for extra flavor)
- 1/2 teaspoon ground ginger (optional)
- Salt and pepper, to taste
- 2 green onions, sliced (for garnish)
- Sesame seeds (optional, for garnish)

Instructions:

1. **Prepare the Cauliflower Rice:**
   - If using a whole head of cauliflower, remove the leaves and stem. Cut it into florets and pulse in a food processor until it resembles rice grains. Alternatively, use pre-riced cauliflower.
2. **Cook the Vegetables:**
   - Heat 1 tablespoon of oil in a large skillet or wok over medium-high heat.
   - Add the diced onion and cook until softened, about 2-3 minutes.
   - Add the garlic and mixed vegetables. Stir-fry for 4-5 minutes, or until the vegetables are tender-crisp.
3. **Scramble the Eggs:**
   - Push the vegetables to one side of the skillet. Add a little more oil if needed.
   - Pour the beaten eggs into the empty side of the skillet and cook, stirring occasionally, until they are just set. Mix the scrambled eggs with the vegetables.
4. **Add the Cauliflower Rice:**
   - Add the riced cauliflower to the skillet with the vegetables and eggs. Stir to combine.
   - Add the soy sauce, hoisin sauce (if using), and ground ginger (if using). Stir well and cook for another 5-7 minutes, or until the cauliflower rice is tender and has absorbed the flavors.
5. **Season and Serve:**
   - Taste and adjust seasoning with salt and pepper if needed.
   - Garnish with sliced green onions and sesame seeds if desired.

Enjoy your Cauliflower Rice Stir-Fry with Eggs as a light and flavorful meal that's both nutritious and satisfying!

Smoked Salmon and Cream Cheese on Whole Grain Bagels

Ingredients:

- 2 whole grain bagels
- 4 tablespoons cream cheese
- 4 ounces smoked salmon
- 1/4 small red onion, thinly sliced
- 1/2 avocado, sliced (optional)
- 1 tablespoon capers (optional)
- Fresh dill or chives, chopped (for garnish)
- Lemon wedges (for serving)

Instructions:

1. **Toast the Bagels:**
   - Slice the whole grain bagels in half and toast them to your preferred level of crispiness.
2. **Spread the Cream Cheese:**
   - Once the bagels are toasted, spread 2 tablespoons of cream cheese on each half.
3. **Assemble the Toppings:**
   - Layer the smoked salmon evenly over the cream cheese on each bagel.
   - Add thin slices of red onion and avocado if using.
   - Top with capers if desired.
4. **Garnish and Serve:**
   - Garnish with fresh dill or chives.
   - Serve with lemon wedges on the side for a fresh squeeze of citrus.

Enjoy your Smoked Salmon and Cream Cheese on Whole Grain Bagels as a delicious and satisfying breakfast or brunch option!

Chickpea and Spinach Stuffed Pita

Ingredients:

- 1 can (15 oz) chickpeas, drained and rinsed
- 2 tablespoons olive oil
- 1 teaspoon ground cumin
- 1/2 teaspoon paprika
- 1/4 teaspoon ground turmeric (optional)
- Salt and pepper, to taste
- 1 cup fresh spinach, chopped
- 1 small red onion, finely diced
- 1/2 cup cherry tomatoes, halved
- 1/4 cup crumbled feta cheese (optional)
- 2 whole wheat pita bread
- 2 tablespoons tahini or yogurt sauce (optional, for drizzling)

Instructions:

1. **Prepare the Chickpeas:**
   - In a medium bowl, toss the chickpeas with olive oil, ground cumin, paprika, turmeric (if using), salt, and pepper.
2. **Cook the Chickpeas:**
   - Heat a skillet over medium heat. Add the spiced chickpeas and cook for 5-7 minutes, stirring occasionally, until they are heated through and slightly crispy.
3. **Prepare the Filling:**
   - In a separate bowl, mix the cooked chickpeas with chopped spinach, diced red onion, cherry tomatoes, and crumbled feta cheese (if using).
4. **Warm the Pita:**
   - Heat the pita bread in a dry skillet or microwave until warm and pliable.
5. **Assemble the Pita:**
   - Cut the pita bread in half to create pockets.
   - Stuff each pita half with the chickpea and spinach mixture.
6. **Add Sauces:**
   - Drizzle with tahini or yogurt sauce if desired.
7. **Serve:**
   - Enjoy immediately as a fresh and satisfying lunch or snack.

This Chickpea and Spinach Stuffed Pita is packed with protein, fiber, and fresh flavors, making it a delicious and nutritious meal!

Sweet Potato and Avocado Breakfast Tacos

Ingredients:

- 1 large sweet potato, peeled and diced
- 1 tablespoon olive oil
- 1/2 teaspoon ground cumin
- 1/2 teaspoon smoked paprika
- Salt and pepper, to taste
- 1 avocado, sliced
- 4 small tortillas (corn or flour)
- 1/2 cup black beans, drained and rinsed (optional)
- 1/4 cup chopped fresh cilantro
- 1/4 cup crumbled feta cheese (optional)
- Lime wedges (for serving)
- Salsa or hot sauce (optional)

Instructions:

1. **Roast the Sweet Potatoes:**
   - Preheat your oven to 400°F (200°C). Toss the diced sweet potato with olive oil, ground cumin, smoked paprika, salt, and pepper.
   - Spread the sweet potatoes on a baking sheet and roast for 25-30 minutes, or until tender and slightly crispy, stirring halfway through.
2. **Warm the Tortillas:**
   - While the sweet potatoes are roasting, warm the tortillas in a dry skillet over medium heat or microwave them until pliable.
3. **Prepare the Toppings:**
   - Slice the avocado and chop the fresh cilantro.
4. **Assemble the Tacos:**
   - Divide the roasted sweet potatoes among the tortillas.
   - Top with avocado slices, black beans (if using), and crumbled feta cheese (if using).
5. **Garnish and Serve:**
   - Sprinkle with fresh cilantro and serve with lime wedges on the side.
   - Add salsa or hot sauce if desired.

Enjoy your Sweet Potato and Avocado Breakfast Tacos as a nutritious and delicious way to start your day!

Greek Salad with Chicken

Ingredients:

- **For the Salad:**
    - 2 cups cooked chicken breast, diced or sliced
    - 4 cups mixed salad greens (e.g., romaine, spinach)
    - 1 cup cherry tomatoes, halved
    - 1 cucumber, sliced
    - 1/2 red onion, thinly sliced
    - 1/2 cup Kalamata olives, pitted
    - 1/2 cup crumbled feta cheese
    - 1/4 cup sliced pepperoncini (optional)
- **For the Dressing:**
    - 1/4 cup olive oil
    - 2 tablespoons red wine vinegar
    - 1 tablespoon lemon juice
    - 1 teaspoon dried oregano
    - 1 clove garlic, minced
    - Salt and pepper, to taste

Instructions:

1. **Prepare the Dressing:**
    - In a small bowl or jar, whisk together the olive oil, red wine vinegar, lemon juice, dried oregano, minced garlic, salt, and pepper.
2. **Assemble the Salad:**
    - In a large salad bowl, combine the mixed greens, cherry tomatoes, cucumber, red onion, olives, and pepperoncini (if using).
    - Add the diced or sliced chicken on top.
    - Sprinkle with crumbled feta cheese.
3. **Dress and Toss:**
    - Drizzle the dressing over the salad and toss gently to combine.
4. **Serve:**
    - Serve immediately, or chill for later.

Enjoy your Greek Salad with Chicken as a refreshing and protein-packed meal!

Apple and Walnut Oat Muffins

Ingredients:

- **Dry Ingredients:**
    - 1 cup rolled oats
    - 1 cup whole wheat flour
    - 1/2 cup chopped walnuts
    - 1/2 cup brown sugar or coconut sugar
    - 1 teaspoon baking powder
    - 1/2 teaspoon baking soda
    - 1 teaspoon ground cinnamon
    - 1/4 teaspoon salt
- **Wet Ingredients:**
    - 1/2 cup unsweetened applesauce
    - 1/2 cup milk (any type; dairy or plant-based)
    - 1/4 cup vegetable oil or melted coconut oil
    - 1 large egg
    - 1 teaspoon vanilla extract
    - 1 medium apple, peeled, cored, and diced (about 1 cup)

Instructions:

1. **Preheat Oven:**
    - Preheat your oven to 350°F (175°C). Line a muffin tin with paper liners or lightly grease it.
2. **Mix Dry Ingredients:**
    - In a large bowl, combine the oats, whole wheat flour, chopped walnuts, brown sugar, baking powder, baking soda, cinnamon, and salt.
3. **Mix Wet Ingredients:**
    - In a separate bowl, whisk together the applesauce, milk, oil, egg, and vanilla extract.
4. **Combine Ingredients:**
    - Pour the wet ingredients into the dry ingredients and stir until just combined. Fold in the diced apple.
5. **Fill Muffin Tin:**
    - Divide the batter evenly among the muffin cups, filling each about 2/3 full.
6. **Bake:**
    - Bake for 20-25 minutes, or until a toothpick inserted into the center of a muffin comes out clean.
7. **Cool:**
    - Allow the muffins to cool in the tin for a few minutes before transferring them to a wire rack to cool completely.

Enjoy your Apple and Walnut Oat Muffins as a nutritious and tasty breakfast or snack!

Spicy Black Bean and Sweet Potato Tacos

Ingredients:

- **For the Filling:**
    - 1 large sweet potato, peeled and diced
    - 1 tablespoon olive oil
    - 1 teaspoon chili powder
    - 1/2 teaspoon cumin
    - 1/2 teaspoon paprika
    - 1/4 teaspoon cayenne pepper (optional, for extra heat)
    - Salt and pepper, to taste
    - 1 can (15 oz) black beans, drained and rinsed
    - 1/2 cup corn kernels (fresh or frozen)
    - 1/2 cup diced red bell pepper
    - 1/2 cup diced red onion
- **For Serving:**
    - 8 small tortillas (corn or flour)
    - 1 avocado, sliced
    - 1 cup shredded lettuce or cabbage
    - 1/2 cup crumbled feta or shredded cheese (optional)
    - Fresh cilantro, chopped (for garnish)
    - Lime wedges (for serving)
    - Salsa or hot sauce (optional)

Instructions:

1. **Roast the Sweet Potatoes:**
    - Preheat your oven to 425°F (220°C). Toss the diced sweet potato with olive oil, chili powder, cumin, paprika, cayenne pepper (if using), salt, and pepper.
    - Spread the sweet potatoes on a baking sheet in a single layer. Roast for 20-25 minutes, or until tender and lightly caramelized, stirring halfway through.
2. **Prepare the Filling:**
    - In a skillet, heat a small amount of olive oil over medium heat. Add the diced red bell pepper and red onion, and cook until softened, about 5 minutes.
    - Stir in the black beans and corn, and cook until heated through. Season with salt and pepper to taste.
3. **Warm the Tortillas:**
    - Warm the tortillas in a dry skillet or microwave them until pliable.
4. **Assemble the Tacos:**
    - Divide the roasted sweet potatoes and black bean mixture among the tortillas.
    - Top with avocado slices, shredded lettuce or cabbage, and crumbled feta or cheese (if using).
5. **Garnish and Serve:**

- Garnish with fresh cilantro and serve with lime wedges and your favorite salsa or hot sauce.

Enjoy your Spicy Black Bean and Sweet Potato Tacos for a satisfying and nutritious meal!

Veggie-Stuffed Omelette

Ingredients:

- 3 large eggs
- 2 tablespoons milk or water
- Salt and pepper, to taste
- 1 tablespoon olive oil or butter
- 1/4 cup diced onion
- 1/4 cup diced bell pepper (any color)
- 1/4 cup diced tomato
- 1/2 cup chopped spinach or kale
- 1/4 cup shredded cheese (optional, e.g., cheddar, feta, or mozzarella)
- 1/4 cup sliced mushrooms (optional)
- Fresh herbs for garnish (optional, e.g., chives, parsley)

Instructions:

1. **Prepare the Vegetables:**
    - Heat olive oil or butter in a non-stick skillet over medium heat.
    - Add the diced onion and cook for about 2 minutes, until softened.
    - Add the diced bell pepper, tomatoes, and mushrooms (if using). Cook for another 2-3 minutes, until the vegetables are tender.
    - Stir in the chopped spinach or kale and cook until wilted. Season with salt and pepper. Remove the vegetables from the skillet and set aside.
2. **Prepare the Egg Mixture:**
    - In a bowl, whisk together the eggs, milk or water, salt, and pepper until well combined.
3. **Cook the Omelette:**
    - In the same skillet, add a little more olive oil or butter if needed. Heat over medium-low.
    - Pour the egg mixture into the skillet, tilting the pan to spread the eggs evenly.
    - Cook undisturbed for about 1-2 minutes, until the edges begin to set but the center is still slightly runny.
4. **Add the Filling:**
    - Spoon the cooked vegetables evenly over one half of the omelette.
    - Sprinkle with shredded cheese if desired.
5. **Fold and Finish:**
    - Carefully fold the other half of the omelette over the filling.
    - Cook for an additional 1-2 minutes, until the cheese is melted (if using) and the omelette is cooked through.
6. **Serve:**
    - Slide the omelette onto a plate and garnish with fresh herbs if desired.

Enjoy your Veggie-Stuffed Omelette as a wholesome and satisfying meal for breakfast, brunch, or even a light dinner!